Mattress Mayhem
Marcy Schaaf
AF490155

In "Mattress Mayhem: Joe's Apple Tree Tumble," join Joe and his brothers on a wild and hilarious adventure! When they stack their mattresses next to the garage for some epic jumps, Joe's excitement leads to an unexpected twist. Jumping off the wrong side of the roof, Joe crashes into a huge apple tree, hitting every branch on the way down. This playful and heartwarming tale of brotherly love and laughter shows that even the craziest mishaps can become cherished memories. Perfect for kids and families, this story highlights the importance of safety, fun, and sticking together.

The four Schaaf brothers
had a great idea.

It's summer, time to make our own fun!

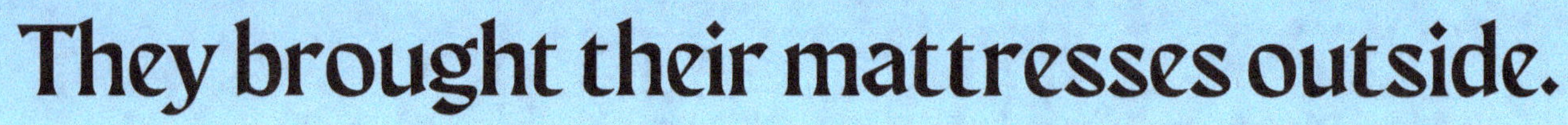
They brought their mattresses outside.

They stacked them high next to the garage.

"Let's jump off the roof!" Joe said excitedly.

One by one, the brothers
climbed up.

Frank jumped first, landing perfectly.

Next, it was Joe's turn to jump.

But Joe got a little mixed up.

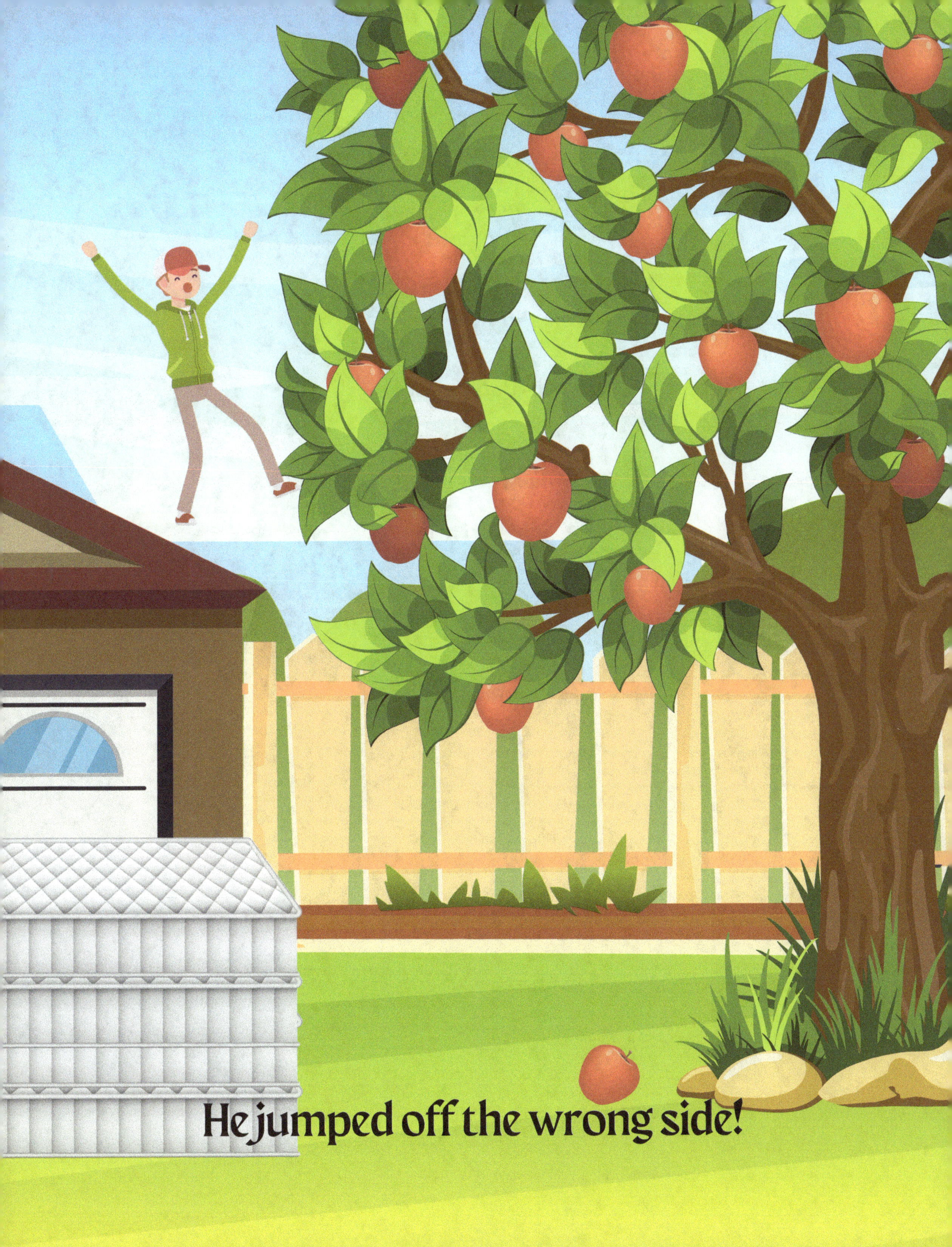

He jumped off the wrong side!

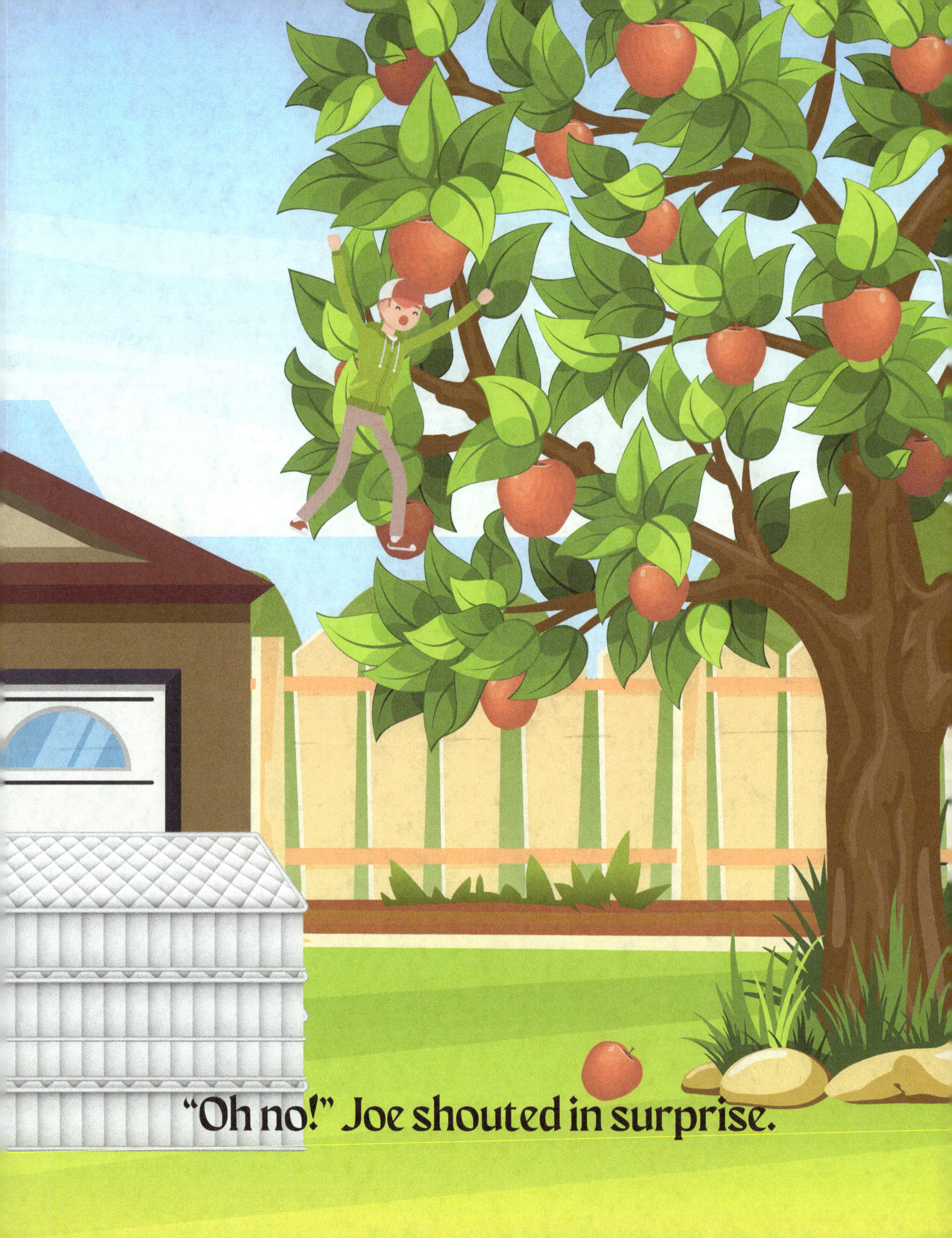

"Oh no!" Joe shouted in surprise.

He crashed right into a huge apple tree.

Branches poked him as he tumbled down.

"Ouch! Ouch! Ouch!" Joe cried loudly.

Finally, he landed with a thud.

The brothers ran to check
on him.

Joe was covered in leaves and apple goo.

"Are you okay, Joe?" Frank asked worriedly.

Joe groaned but then laughed.

"That was one wild ride!" he chuckled.

They dusted him off .

"Next time, stick to our side!" said
Frank.

Joe nodded, still smiling brightly.

They all laughed about the crazy
adventure.

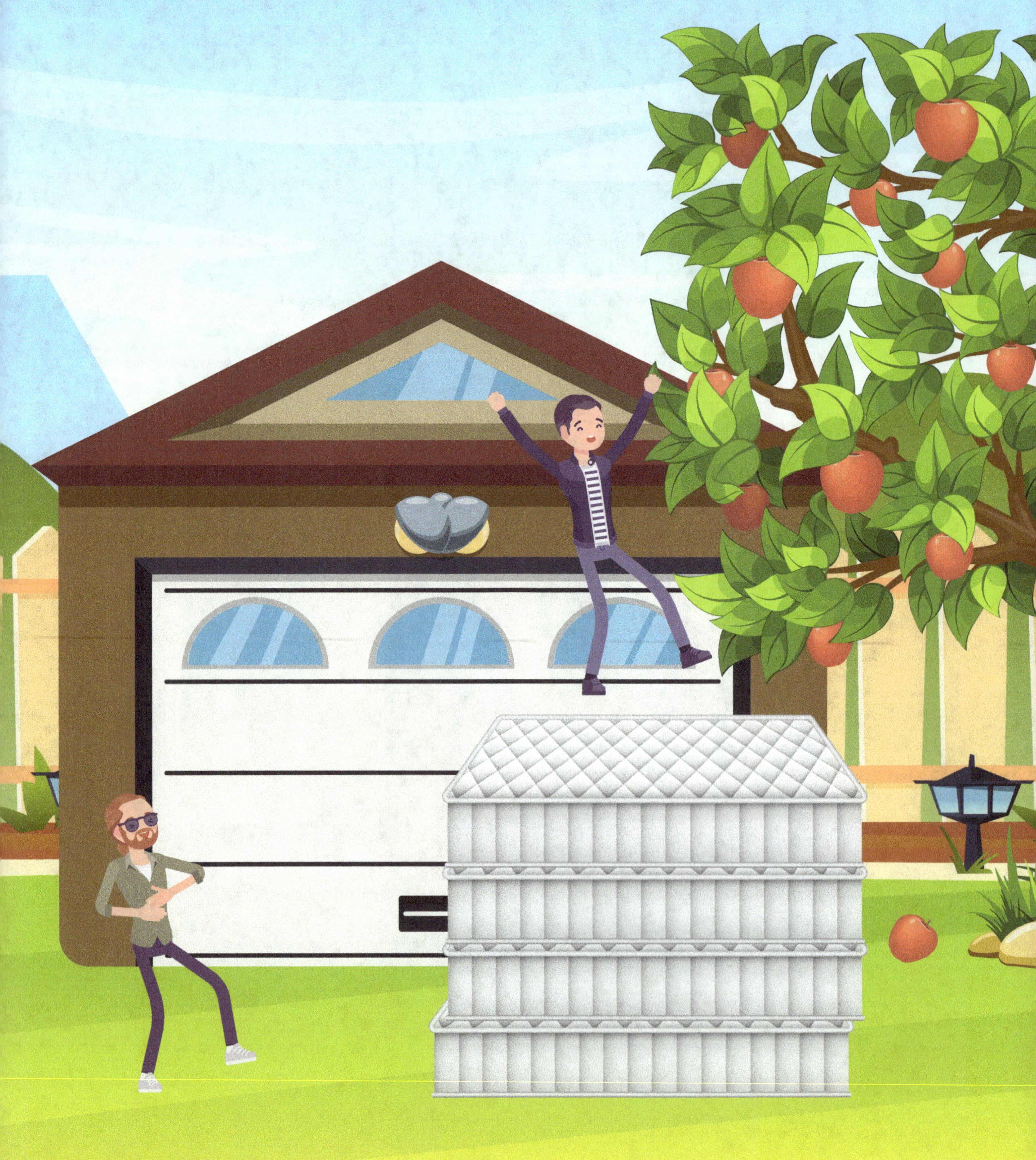
Joe and his brothers had lots of fun.

They learned to jump safely together.

Brotherly love made everything better.

The end.

Books By Schaaf

www.BookBySchaaf.com

find us at:

Available at
amazon